In-line Skating

Chuck Miller

Steadwell Books

Raintree Steck-Vaughn Publishers

A Harcourt Company

Austin · New York
www.raintreesteckvaughn.com

Published by Raintree Steck-Vaughn Publishers, an imprint of Steck-Vaughn Company.

Library of Congress Cataloging-in-Publication Data
Miller, Chuck.
    In-line skating/Chuck Miller.
        p. cm.-- (Extreme sports)
    Includes bibliographical references (p.) and index.
    Summary: Discusses the history, techniques, and equipment of in-line skating and explains how to get started and how to compete.
    ISBN 0-7398-4688-4
    1. In-line skating--Juvenile literature [1.In-line skating.] I. Title. II. Extreme sports (Austin, Tex.)

GV859.73 M547 2001
796.21--dc21   2001019826

Printed and bound in the United States of America
1 2 3 4 5 6 7 8 9 10 WZ 05 04 03 02 01

Produced by Compass Books

Photo Acknowledgments
Tony Donaldson: title page, 8, 12, 17, 18, 21, 28, 30, 32, 39, 40, 42 top, 42 bottom, 43 top, 43 bottom; Jack Gescheidt: 4-5, 6, 14-15, 22, 24-25, 27, 34, 36; Aneal N. Vohra , Unicorn Stock Photos: cover

Content Consultant
Kristine M. Simeone
Director, In-line Certification Program
International In-line Skating Association

Contents

Introduction 5

How To Use This Book 6

In-line Skating 9

What Safe Skaters Do 10

What You Need to Start 14

Who Can Become an In-line Skater? 25

Who are the Professional In-line Skaters? . .33

Competing in In-line Skating 37

Quick Facts About In-line Skating 42

Glossary 44

Internet Sites and Addresses 46

Books to Read 47

Index 48

In-line skaters seeks thrills by jumping off objects and doing tricks in the air.

Introduction

In-line skating is an extreme sport that is growing more and more popular. In-line skaters ride on skates that have rows of wheels in a straight line underneath them. They often use **ramps** and obstacles to do tricks. Extreme sports are relatively new sports taken up by daring athletes. Along with the fun of extreme sports, however, comes the risk of injury. People who participate in extreme sports must do everything they can to be safe.

You have probably heard of the **X Games**. But do you know what a **half-pipe** is? Do you know how the roller skate led to the invention of the in-line skate? Who are the top in-line skaters in the word today? What do you need to do if you want to take up the sport? This book will answer all of these questions and more.

> In-line skaters ride on sidewalks and
> paths in cities around the world.

How To Use This Book

This book is divided into parts called chapters. The
title of the chapter tells you what it is about. The list
of chapters and their page numbers appear on the
Table of Contents on page 3. The Index on page 48

gives you page numbers where you can find important topics discussed in this book.

Each chapter has colorful photographs, captions, and side-bars. The photographs show you things written about in the book, so you will know what they look like. A caption is an explanation that tells you about the photograph. The captions in this book are in light blue boxes. Side-bars give you extra information about the subject.

You may not know what some of the words in this book mean. To learn new words, you look them up in a dictionary. This book has a dictionary called a glossary. Words that appear in boldface type are in the Glossary on page 44.

You can use the Internet sites listed on page 46 to learn more about topics discussed in this book. You can write letters to the addresses of organizations listed on page 46, asking them questions or to send you helpful information.

This is pro in-line skater Matt Selerno at a competition doing tricks that are scored by judges.

In-line Skating

In-line skating is a cross between ice skating and roller skating. Most in-line skates contain four wheels in a single row. This allows in-line skaters to move over smooth surfaces like ice skaters move over ice. In-line skaters often ride on streets and sidewalks. They need to stay away from dangers, including cars, bicycles, and other people.

In-line skating is one of the fastest growing sports in North America. In 1993, there were about 13 million in-line skaters in the United States. By 1999, that number had grown to more than 32 million.

What Safe Skaters Do

The International In-line Skating Association (IISA) was founded in 1991 by skaters and skate makers. It teaches people how to skate safely. It says safe skaters should do the following five things.

1. Skaters should skate smart and follow **traffic** laws.

2. Skaters should always wear **helmets** and pads, which must be in good shape.

3. Skaters need to stop and turn safely.

4. Skaters must follow the same traffic laws as cars and bikes.

5. Skaters should be polite to other skaters and also to people walking on the sidewalk. Skaters should pass other skaters only on the left. Before passing another skater, yell "passing on your left." Skaters should stop to let people walking on the street go by them.

...e Skating

...y kinds of in-line skating.
...ers enter races, like runners do.
...te on closed-off roads. Others,
...aters, skate around a track.
...e skaters play roller hockey. The
...ce hockey on in-line skates. Roller
...layed on a flat area of ground, such
...ty parking lot, with a hockey stick
...all instead of a puck.

...line skaters who do tricks are called
...gressive skaters. They use ramps or **street courses** to do tricks. Street courses are special places made for in-line skaters. They have stairs, street curbs, and railings for trick skating.

> These in-line skaters are playing roller hockey on their skates.

How In-line Skating Began

A Belgian man named John Joseph Merlin was the first person to make a roller skate. In 1760, he put wooden spools on his shoes. His skates did not work well. He could not steer or stop. When he tried to show his friends how they worked, he skated into a mirror.

In 1863, a man from New York named James L. Plimpton made skates that worked better. He put four wooden wheels on each of his shoes. He then put rubber over each wheel. The skates turned easily, but they could not stop well.

In 1960, the Chicago Skate company built an in-line skate. It was not easy to stay up on, and it was hard to stop because it did not have a good brake. In 1979, a Minnesota man named Scott Olson saw a used pair of these skates at a local store. He thought he could use the skates in the summer to train for ice skating.

Olson put better wheels and good brakes on the skates. This made them easier to steer and stop. In 1980, Olson and his brother, Brennan, started making their own skates. They started the Rollerblade company. Other companies began making in-line skates, too. More and more people began using them instead of roller skates. Skaters found that in-line skates allowed them to go faster and to turn more easily.

What You Need to Start

Helmets and pads protect skaters when they fall. They are as important as skates. All young skaters should wear a helmet and pads whenever they skate.

A helmet is designed to protect a skater's head if he or she falls. A helmet should fit well. Most helmets have a soft inner **shell** and a harder outer shell. Helmets should be approved by such safety groups as the International In-line Skating Association (IISA).

Skaters should wear elbow and knee pads to protect their skin and bones. These pads should be soft on the inside with a hard shell on the outside. As with a helmet, pads need to fit well. If they do not, they can slip off during a fall.

Smart, experienced in-line skaters always wear a helmet to protect their heads.

Wrist Guards

Skaters injure their hands and wrists more than any other parts of their bodies. **Wrist guards** keep a skater's wrists straight during a fall. This lessens the chance that skaters will injure their wrists. An injury is some kind of hurt or damage, such as broken bones or a sprain. A sprain means one of the body's joints has been twisted, tearing the muscles or ligaments. A ligament holds together the bones in a joint.

Skates

A good skate is a safe skate. Some in-line skates cost less than others do. Most inexpensive skates, however, are not comfortable and are not easy to steer, which makes them less safe. Skaters could injure themselves using these skates. Sporting goods

Skater Profile: Cesar Mora

Cesar Mora is known as one of the best in-line skaters in the world. He was born in Sydney, Australia in 1974. He won a gold medal in the X Games in 1998 and he won the Aggressive Skaters Association World In-line Championships later that year. Mora likes to teach other in-line skaters new tricks.

stores will sometimes sell good used skates for less money than new ones. These skates are usually safe and work well.

All in-line skates are made up of the same parts. The hard outside covering on a skate is called the shell. The shell covers the **boot**, which is the body of the skate.

This is pro in-line skater Chris Edwards using aggressive skates to do tricks.

Liners, Frames, Wheels

A **liner** is often inside the boot. The liner is like a thick sock made of foam. The **frame** connects the wheels to the boot. Frames are made of plastic or metal.

Wheels are one of the most important parts of a skate. In-line skate wheels are made of hard rubber. Skaters choose their wheels based on size and hardness.

Choosing the Right Skate

Choosing the right skate is important for safety. Most in-line skaters buy fitness skates. These have a hard outer shell and four large wheels. They can be used for many different kinds of skating. Some skaters need to use special skates. Using the wrong skate for certain types of skating can be dangerous.

Timeline

1760: John Joseph Merlin puts wooden spools on his shoes
1863: James L. Plimpton invents a skate with rubber-covered wheels
1960: Chicago Skate builds the first in-line skate
1980: Scott and Brendan Olson start the Rollerblade company
1995: The X Games begin

Kinds of Skates

Aggressive skates are designed to handle the stress of stunts and tricks. These skates have hard plastic or leather shells that cover the boot. They have thicker liners than fitness skates. They have four wheels, but these wheels are smaller than the ones on fitness skates. This makes the skates easier to steer.

Artistic skates are used for dancing. The boots are much like ice-skate boots. They have three small wheels. The front and back wheels have a different hardness than the middle wheel. This allows skaters to turn and spin smoothly.

Hockey skates are most often made of leather and are tied with shoestrings. The shoestrings give a tighter fit. Hockey skates have four small wheels to make them easy to steer.

Speed skates have five large wheels. This helps

Did You Know?

Did you know what group of people in Pennsylvania ride in-line skates? The Dutch Amish people do. Who are the Dutch Amish? They are people who live a simple kind of life. They do not use cars or telephones or television. They do, however, ride in-line skates.

▲ **This is pro skater Fabiola Da Silva doing a trick at the top of a half-pipe ramp.**

skaters go faster. These skates are not for beginners. They have no brake and are hard to turn.

Ramps and the Street

Some in-line skaters do tricks on ramps and street courses. They may do tricks on the ground or in the air. Tricks done in the air are called **aerials**. Most aerials are done using ramps.

 This is what an in-line skating course at the X Games looks like from above.

Doing Tricks

In-line skaters use three kinds of ramps for tricks. One is the **quarter-pipe.** It has one curved wall. Another ramp is the half-pipe. It has two curved walls and is shaped like a "U." The third kind of ramp is the spine ramp. It is made by placing two half-pipe ramps back to back.

In-line skaters once did tricks on streets, sidewalks, and in parks. Many people thought this was dangerous for skaters, for people walking, and for people driving. Many towns made laws to stop skaters from doing tricks in public places.

Skaters began practicing tricks on street courses. These have steps, street curbs, and railings. Many also have ramps. Many towns now have these courses made just for people who do extreme sports.

Race Tracks

In-line racing began in the 1980s. Most in-line racers skate around an oval **track**. These racers are called speed skaters. Today, most speed skaters race distances of 328 to 656 feet (100 to 200 m).

Some speed skaters race on road courses. Public roads are blocked off during these races. They cover very long distances.

Downhill in-line skaters race each other down steep hills. This is very dangerous. Downhill in-line skaters earn their living from prize money they win while racing.

In-line skaters should always wear clothing
that will protect them if they fall.

Who Can
Become an In-line Skater?

Almost anyone can start skating if he or she is prepared. It helps to be in good physical shape. Before beginning, new skaters need to buy the right skates and learn the safety rules. Then, they must learn how to skate.

Stretching

Skaters use many muscles in their bodies, so stretching before skating is important. Skaters who stretch do not get injured as often. They also will feel more rested and awake while skating. Skaters should stretch their arms, legs, and backs before skating.

Skills to Learn

New skaters need to practice a few moves the first time out. They should find a flat piece of ground where they can learn how to stand while on skates. They should stand with their feet shoulder-width apart. Their skates should point straight in front of them. The rest of the body should point straight ahead, too. Skaters must keep their heads up at all times to see what is in front of them.

Skater Profile: Matt Salerno

Matt Salerno is a good friend of Cesar Mora. He also was born in Sydney, Australia. In 1997, he won a gold medal at the X Games. In 1998, he won a silver medal at the X Games.

This in-line skater at the X Games has used a quarter-pipe ramp to go upside down.

> Beginning skaters go to competitions to
> watch Cesar Mora, above, doing tricks
> on half-pipe ramps.

Starting and Stopping

A good first move for new skaters is to push off
with the left foot. Skaters will then shift the weight to
the right foot, rolling on that foot. Next, they will
bring the left foot next to, and just ahead of, the right
foot. The skater will do this move again the other

way, pushing off with the right foot and rolling on the left foot.

New skaters have to learn how to stop using the heel brake. Most in-line skates have a heel brake on the right skate. Skaters should move the brake to the left skate if that is more comfortable. To stop, skaters put the skate with the heel brake forward while moving. Skaters then point the toe of that skate upward until the brake touches the ground.

New skaters often turn by moving their legs far apart. Their bodies looks like the capital letter "A" when they do this. Skaters put their body weight on the skate opposite of the way they want to turn. This will make their skates turn in the direction they want.

When falling, skaters should land first on their knees, then on their elbows, always falling forward. They should land on their wrists last, and then make their bodies flat. They should slide along the ground with their skates pointed up. Falling this way helps skaters scrape their pads instead of their skin.

This beginning skater has learned basic skills and is trying them on a road where there is no traffic.

Where Can I Train?

Taking lessons from an in-line skating teacher is a good idea. They can teach the rules of skating. They can watch skaters and show them how to skate better. They can teach people what to wear when skating. They can show new skaters how to repair their skates.

The best group to contact to find a skating teacher is the International In-line Skating Association. It has helped more than 2,000 people become skating teachers since 1991. These teachers can teach many types of in-line skating, including aggressive skating, speed skating, and roller hockey.

Skater Profile: Sam Fogerty

Sam Fogarty was voted the best overall aggressive in-line skater on the 1999 Aggressive Skating Association Pro Tour. Fogarty, 19, was born in Melbourne, Australia, and won a silver medal in the 1999 ASA World Championships.

Professional in-line skater Aaron Feinberg is doing a trick on a rail.

Who are the Professional In-line Skaters?

Fabiola Da Silva began skating in competitions in 1996. She is a **professional**. In her first three years, she won three gold medals in the X Games. These games were started in 1995 by the television network ESPN. They have become the best-known competition for all kinds of extreme sports. Da Silva also won a gold medal at the 2000 X Games. Today, Da Silva is one of the most famous skaters in the world. She is often ranked by the ASA as the best woman skater.

Aaron Feinberg is one of the best street-course skaters in the world. Feinberg won the men's in-line street finals at the X Games when he was only 16. Feinberg was born in Portland, Oregon in 1981. He ranks high on the ASA Pro Tour and is considered one of the top five aggressive in-line skaters in the world.

> **These in-line skaters are racing on a road course.**

Practice

Like anyone else, Da Silva and Feinberg had to learn how to skate. They began with the basics, then practiced easy tricks, and then more difficult ones. Today, Da Silva and Feinberg make up new tricks of their own. These new tricks help them win competitions. Each new trick takes more practice and more hard work.

How to Ride the Ramp

Skaters begin by skating across the ramp to build speed. Then they skate up the wall of the ramp and jump into the air at the top. Skaters try to jump as high as they can. They call this "catching air." Skaters often grab their legs when doing aerials.

Street Courses

Street skaters also use small ramps to do aerials. They do **grinds** by jumping up onto railings or street curbs. They drag the wheels or frames of their skates across the railing or curb. They put **grind plates** on their skates to grind better. These are metal or plastic plates on the inside of skate frames.

Skater Profile: Chris Edwards

Chris Edwards is often called the father of aggressive in-line skating. He invented many of the tricks used by aggressive skaters today. He began skating in competitions in the mid-1990s. He has won many competitions, including the gold medal in the X Games. In 1998, Edwards broke his arm and missed the entire skating season. The next year, he began skating in competitions again. He now competes less, and, instead, teaches others how to skate.

This skater at the X Games has used a ramp to catch big air and do a trick.

Competing in In-line Skating

The Aggressive Skaters Association (ASA) is the only international aggressive in-line skating group. It was founded in 1994 by a group of in-line skaters. Anyone can belong.

The ASA runs the ASA Pro Tour. More than 150 skaters from more than 20 countries skate for prizes and money. ASA competitions include the ASA World Championships and the ESPN X Games.

Becoming a skater on the ASA Pro Tour is not easy. To do so, skaters must do well on the ASA amateur tour. Amateur skaters are those who skate not for money but for fun. Amateurs must reach the national competitions in their home countries. If they win, they move on to international competitions, where the best skaters may make the ASA Pro Tour. In 1999, more than 7,000 amateur skaters competed for 30 open spots on the ASA Pro Tour.

Sponsors

Most skaters on the ASA Pro Tour make their living from skating. They skate in ASA competitions year-round. They are ranked on their performances. The top-ranked skaters compete in the X Games and World In-line Championships.

Competing in so many events involves a lot of travel and costs a lot of money. Most skaters could not do it without **sponsors**. A sponsor is a company that pays a skater to use or advertise its product. One such sponsor is Rollerblade, which sponsors Fabiola Da Silva. Rollerblade pays her to wear its skates.

Judging a Trick

In-line skaters have a set amount of time to skate in street competitions. Judges give them points for tricks. Harder tricks get more points. Judges also give points for style and for the number of obstacles skaters use.

In-line skaters also have a set amount of time to skate in ramp competitions. Judges give points for the number of tricks they do. Harder trick get the most points. Judges also give extra points to those who catch the most air.

This in-line skater is racing down a course on a dirt hill.

In-line skating is becoming popular for people of all ages.

Competitions and Prizes

The X Games began in 1995. The television network ESPN has held and shown these games each year since then. Many different extreme sports are performed at the X Games. In-line skating competitions include men's and women's ramp events and men's and women's street events. Skaters compete for gold, silver, and bronze medals, and also for prize money.

Skaters who make the ASA Pro Tour also compete for prize money. In 2000, ASA professionals competed for more than $700,000 in prize money.

In-line skating competitions are popular all over the world. Skaters are always making up new tricks. Skate makers are also making better skates. In-line skating remains one of the fastest growing sports in North America. It is the combined effort of people of all ages that makes it such a popular sport.

Quick Facts About
In-line Skating

Dave Cooper and Eddie Matzger in-line skated up and down Mount Kilimanjaro, Africa's highest mountain, in 1998.

About half of in-line skaters are women.

About half of in-line skaters are 18 years of age or older.

Some skiers practice skiing down steep hills on their in-line skates.

An in-line skater can burn 285 calories in 30 minutes and produce a heart rate of 148 beats per minute.

Skating fast one minute and then skating slow for one minute can burn 450 calories if you skate for 30 minutes.

Eito and Takeshi Yasutoko are brothers. In 2000, Eito won an X Games gold medal while Takeshi won a silver.

More than 40,000 fans watched the 1998 ASA Pro and Amateur Championships in Las Vegas.

Skate wheels have a longer life if they are regularly rotated.

43

Glossary

aerial (AIR-ee-uhl)—a trick done while in the air

boot (BOOT)—the main body of an in-line skate

frame (FRAYM)—the part of a skate that connects the wheels to the skate

grind (GRINDE)—to drag a skate across a street curb or railing

grind plates (GRINDE PLAYTS)—metal or plastic plates attached to the frames of aggressive in-line skates

half-pipe (HAF PIPE)—a U-shaped ramp with two curved walls

helmet (HEL-mit)—a hard kind of hat that protects a person's head

liner (LINE-ur)—the inside of an in-line skate boot

professional (pruh-FESH-uh-nuhl)—a person who makes money doing something others do for fun

quarter-pipe (KWOR-tur PIPE)—a ramp with one curved wall

ramp (RAMP)—a curved surface used for freestyle tricks

shell (SHEL)—the hard outer case of an in-line skate boot

sponsor (SPON-sur)—a company that pays someone to use what it sells or to advertise its product

street course (STREET KORSS)—a group of ramps, street curbs, stairs, and railings used for tricks

track (TRAK)—a course for racing on

traffic (TRAF-ik)—car, bicycles, and people traveling on streets or sidewalks

wrist guard (RIST GARD)—an item worn to protect the hand and wrist

X Games (EKS GAYMZ)—a popular extreme sports competition hosted by the sports television network ESPN

Internet Sites and Addresses

About.com: In-line Skating
http://in-lineskating.about.com

Aggressive Skaters Association (ASA)
http://www.aggroskate.com

ESPN: Extreme Sports
http://www.expn.go.com/extreme

International In-line Skating Association (IISA)
http://www.iisa.org

Skate FAQs
http://www.skatefaq.com

Women's Aggressive Skating Network
http://www.xtremecentral.com/WASN/WASNintro.htm

Aggressive Skaters Association
13468 Beach Avenue
Marina Del Rey, CA 90292

Canadian In-line and Roller Skating Association
679 Queens Quay West
Unit 117
Toronto, ON M5V 3A9
Canada

International In-line Skating Association
105 South Seventh Street
Wilmington, NC 28401

USA Hockey In-line
4965 North 30th Street
Colorado Springs, CO 80919

USA In-line Racing
1271 Boynton Street #15
Glendale, CA 91025

46

Books to Read

Edwards, Chris. *The Young In-line Skater.* New York: DK Publishing, 2000. This book presents basic information on the essential skills, techniques, and equipment for the sport of in-line skating.

Kaminker, Laura. *In-line Skating!* Get Aggressive. New York: Rosen Central, 1999. This book introduces the sport of aggressive in-line skating, discussing its development, equipment, basic moves, and safety tips.

Miller, Liz. *Get Rolling: The Beginner's Guide to In-line Skating.* New York: McGraw Hill, 1998. This book gives a overview of methods, equipment, and safety for new skaters.

Sullivan, George. *In-line Skating: A Complete Guide for Beginners.* New York: Puffin, 1993. This book discusses many ways for those new to the sport to use and enjoy in-line skates.

Index

aerial, 21, 35

boot, 17, 19, 20

frame, 19, 35

grind, 35
grind plates, 35

half-pipe, 5, 22
helmet, 10, 14

ice skating, 9, 13

liner, 19, 20

North America, 9, 41

professional, 33, 41

quarter-pipe, 22

ramp, 5, 11, 21-23, 35, 38, 41
Rollerblade, 13, 19, 29, 38
roller hockey, 11, 31
roller skating, 9

shell, 14, 17, 19, 20
speed skate, 11, 21, 23
sponsor, 38
street course, 11, 21, 23, 35

track, 11, 23
traffic, 10

wrist guard, 16

X Games, 5, 16, 19, 26, 33, 35, 37, 38, 41, 43